Praise f

“Music Xray provides a ... s,
music executives, and t ... sic
Xray, my team and I are able to constantly ...
ready to take the next steps to advance their careers and this book is a great resource to help artists have a better shot at success.”
Eddie Caldwell - Music of the Sea
(Has placed Music Xray artists' music in MTV's “Real World”, Scary Movie 5, Rock Star Energy Drink ads, and ABC's “Scandal”, and many others.)

“Music Xray is an incredible A&R tool that gives unsigned artists a chance to be heard. The direct connection to gate keepers and decision maker's are what set this platform apart from the rest. **Maximizing Music Xray** breaks down the proven methods to not only advance on Music Xray, but also in the music business. A must-read for any unsigned act looking for a chance to take their career up a notch.”
Eric McLellan - Director of A&R Sire Records - Warner Music Group

“Music Xray, it's a great tool for any artist. As an A&R rep it enables me to interact with artists from around the world I normally wouldn't have the chance to be in contact with. It provides artists with the opportunity to receive direct feedback that is usually reserved for artists we are in negotiations with. This book gives artists a real look at how the industry evaluates new songs and talent.”
Fred Hanba - A&R - Tommy Boy Entertainment

“I have used other platforms/vehicles to get Lions Named Leo's name “out there” and further our musical goals, however, they all really fall short of Music Xray.

As a musician and just as a regular guy, I love Mr. Dolph's honest and understandable approach to his book. He explains the process very well and backs it up with realities. Artists, make sure you have good, well recorded material and CHOOSE YOUR OPPORTUNITIES WISELY! I love the book and love Music Xray!

In today's music biz it's nice to have Music Xray legitimately “leveling the playing field”.
Rob Saranpa *of the band* **Lions Named Leo**

What key music buyers say about **Music Xray**

"I prefer to manage music submission with Music Xray because of the easy accessibility of the site. In doing what I do, I have people sending me music from all over and in a variety of formats, from CD to MP3. With Music Xray I can access my submissions from wherever I am in the world, and I have a clean record of songs I have accepted, as well as communications that I have started."
Cliff Audretch, Sr. Director A&R / Staff Producer, Show Dog (Universal Music Group).

"I love it! Music Xray has been an integral A&R scouting source for my operation and I always look forward to reviewing the material from artists, writers, managers."
Jake Livingston, Senior Director, Creative at Primary Wave, former A&R Epic Records (Sony)

"Music Xray is a great tool for artists to be heard by the industry and this book lays out how artists and songwriters can put their best foot forward."
Dallas Martin, A&R Atlantic Records

"Music Xray provides a unique avenue for artists to get music heard by execs and people that can help their careers. As a Multi-Platinum A&R Exec / Producer/Writer, when I listen to the submissions and find qualities I believe I can work with, it's magic! I found two such artists & was able to develop them, shop them, and get them major label record & publishing deals, film & TV placements, tours, managers, agents etc. ...Music Xray allows it to happen and this book will help you chart your course."
Jeff Blue - signed Macy Grey, Linkin Park, Hoobastank, Daniel Powter, Limp Bizkit, Korn, and The Last Goodnight while senior A&R executive at Warner Bros. Records, Interscope Records, Virgin/Capitol Music Group, Sony/BMG/Jive Records, Atlantic Records, and RCA/J Records

What is Music Xray and how can it help you?

Music Xray levels the playing field for musicians, songwriters, and bands when it comes to getting access to industry decision makers.

Get your music to any of Music Xray's 1200+ Music Industry Professional members (MIPs). Music Xray guarantees that they listen and respond or your money back. If your song gets good ratings from a few industry professionals, Music Xray's sophisticated filtering process will get it shown to many more professionals at no additional cost.

On Music Xray, the cream rises to the top quickly. And if your music isn't what the industry is currently seeking, Music Xray puts you in touch with established industry veterans who can offer career coaching and professional song critiques.

How is Music Xray different?

- No annual membership fees! You only pay for the opportunities you select.
- No Pre-Screeners! Your track goes directly to the Industry Professional.
- Money back, 45 day listen and response guarantee! Submit with confidence.

The Author

Norman Dolph, is a long time lyric writer, producer of Andy Warhol's Banana Album, "The Velvet Underground & Nico". Founder of New York's First Mobile Disco. Former board member of AGAC - American Guild of Authors and Composers, (now SGA - Songwriter's Guild of America). Writer member of ASCAP. Publisher member of ASCAP, BMI and NMPA - National Music Publisher's Association. Forty year voting member of NARAS The Grammy Organization. He has written and listened to a lot of songs.

He has USED Music Xray. Both as a writer and a MIP (Music Industry Professional). He has much to say that will help you get your songs actually HEARD by people who matter. He's got even more to say about how to get your GOOD SONGS actually bought! ... Using Music Xray. -- The sharpest new tool in the songwriter's kit.

GoodReadBooks™, Inc.
"Reading Is Time Well Spent"

Maximizing Music Xray
Pitch Your Songs DIRECTLY To Music Industry Pros!

For information, contact: Service@GoodReadBooks.com

First Printing
Published New York City, NY, USA

Catalog Information:

Author: Dolph, Norman
Music Xray - Songwriting - Music Business - Recordings - Music Industry

Title: Maximizing Music Xray
Subtitle: Pitch Your Songs DIRECTLY To Music Industry Pros!

ISBN: 978-0-9777512-2-8 (Trade Paperback Edition)
ISBN: 978-0-0777512-3-5 (Amazon Kindle Edition)

6 5 4 3 2 1

MAXIMIZING MUSIC XRAY

Pitch Your Songs
DIRECTLY
To Music Industry Pros!

By

Norman Dolph

TABLE OF CONTENTS

READ ME FIRST!

GET THE MOST FROM YOUR MUSIC XRAY DOLLAR

The first thing I'm going to tell you is something you already know:

If you are a songwriter,

... you are gonna get REJECTED.

More Accurately:

SOME or ALL of the songs you write are going to be rejected MOST of the time by MANY PEOPLE.

This would be true for Sammy Kahn, Stevie Wonder, Sting, and Paul Simon. It was probably true even for Stephen Foster.

Most people will reject most of your stuff. The object is to find the **one** guy in the pipeline who:

1. Loves your song(s), and
2. Is in a position to do something about it.

There are several ways to attempt this. You've probably tried at least 3 or 4 by now. Here we'll focus on a program that is probably the straightest, most legit, transparent, and dare I say "effective" of all, **Music Xray**.

With this warning: If your song sucks – it will get rejected.

And, as in the real world: **Your song is up against a WORLD of good competition,** strong songs written by writers as talented and motivated as you are, maybe more so. If your song is merely nice, good, OK, and your wife, "Loves it!" – **it will probably get rejected** – because the bar is high.

The bar is high because of the investment the Buyer must make in your song. A song needs to get 2 to 5 million YouTube views just to recoup that investment.

The bar is high because in the days of Brian Wilson and Mick Jagger, a town had 3 or maybe 4 radio stations. Everybody was focused on relatively few, relatively slow-moving targets. There were no Smartphones, no ear buds, no Spotify, no Pandora, no YouTube; everybody had the same few choices. Now, everybody has an infinity of choices.

Getting somebody to choose your stuff out of the song-swamp requires that your stuff be really, really good.

SO:

If you get rejected, it is not you personally. It's not that your music is bad; it's just that your music isn't colossal — at least in the set of ears making the evaluation.

And further:

Much great music gets rejected - SIMPLY BECAUSE OF TIMING. The perfect artist for your song just finished an album and is touring for 7 months. Another perfect artist just changed styles,"went acoustic", went into a coma, released a song with a title like yours. Etc., etc., etc. — you lose your shot.

For every 100 weak songs, rejected because they are weak, one sensational song will get rejected simply because the timing is not right.

If you're still with me, **I proffer that Music Xray, dollar for dollar, is the best money you can spend on the problem of CONNECTING your SONG to EARS that can advance it along the trail.**

Worldwide, there are many users of music who aggressively seek to **license** music for specific uses. **If it's your music, you get the fee**.

This may not fill your immediate dream of "Katy Perry's next release", but a few hundred here, a few thousand there, will keep you in ink and score paper till you write the big one.

Licensing for TV, Motion Pictures, Commercials, and Online uses represents a big fraction of Music Xray's opportunities.

Ironically, compared to the cost of demos, software, studio time etc., dollars spent on finding a market with **Music Xray** (**"MXR"**), aren't that much. Some complain that MXR isn't "free". The Buyers you are trying to reach are swarmed-on by hundreds of writers; via email, snail mail, elevator pitches, helium balloons... every possible scheme and scam.

At least with MXR the convention is clear. A slight $ barrier to entry is created to discourage and skim off 80% of the wannabes, those who only want a free ride and who pollute the listener's attention. The Buyer agrees to devote his full and honest attention to those submissions which come in via MXR. And in that filtered, refined universe, the very best songs which fit the timing and the specs of the request will get selected.

Better you compete against a few other great songs, than get lost in an inbox soup of hundreds of mind-numbing, mediocre songs.

MXR is not perfect, but it's stable and evolving all the time. Ideally it should become the Airbnb of the music business. Buyer and seller meet — **when requirements match desires, the deal is done.**

AND remember, Music Xray does not siphon off any part of the revenue of whatever deal you make with your buyer. You and the buyer exchange phone numbers, and MXR is out of the transaction thereafter.

Enough backgrounder.

Long Story Short: You've looked realistically at your catalog, and you've selected the very strongest material. Now...

How do you put Music Xray to work for you, to reduce the chances of rejection, by increasing your chances of success?

Stay tuned.

I. BASIC UNDERSTANDINGS

A quick review before we start:

- This is not a book about how to write a song.
- It's about how to **USE** Music Xray ("**MXR**").
- It is a book about how to increase the odds of getting picked up by a Music Industry Professional ("**MIP**") on MXR.
- This book is PRIMARILY aimed at writers who want to get their SONGS placed. It is SECONDARILY aimed at performers who want to place themselves as ARTISTS.
- First requirement: Your song must not suck.
- If it does suck, you waste your money. You can't use MXR to finesse a lame effort onto the market. Refine. Rewrite. Fix. Or scrap it and write a better one.
- Strange as it seems - **MXR profits more by your NOT submitting weak songs,** than by your blasting some less-than-well-done effort all over, just to see if something sticks. **Why?**

- Because if you do this:
    - It's unlikely you will sell your song, you'll get discouraged, blame the conduit, leave the process, and MXR loses a customer.
    - The professional ears will get deadened and will either raise the fee to tune out the noise – which negatively affects ALL writers – or limit the opportunities. This helps nobody.
    - If you get discouraged and exit, then you deprive yourself of feedback, coaching, and the learning you get from rejection. (Trust me – you <u>do</u> learn.)
- Better you fire off a FEW, well aimed, well timed, well polished bullets, than attempt to carpet-bomb every ear in the potential audience.

- Luckily, there are plenty of coaches. Some songs need only a polish, others an overhaul, and yet others, a gentle but firm suggestion that the effort is better spent elsewhere.

- Look at it this way, there are thousands of writers out there with the potential to write at least one terrific song. EVERYBODY - the writer, the buyer, and MXR - benefits if that song can be nurtured, matured, and guided from the writer's pen into a sync license or released recording.

- MXR's process is designed to focus the writer on the "great", not the "many".

- To reduce wasting time with sucky songs, start in by reading: *The Lefsetz Letter*. Free, sobering, and **vital** to today's music situation. Especially the archives:

  www.lefsetz.com/lists/?p=subscribe&id=1

  Read 20 or 30 issues. Seriously – stop now and read some Lefsetz, then think over where you are and where you're going.

- Other resources for the active writer:

  ASCAP's Daily Brief:
  http://www.magnetmail.net/actions/subscription_form_ascap.cfm

  Songwriters Guild of America website:
  www.songwritersguild.com/

  Music Think Tank:
  http://www.musicthinktank.com//

  Music Industry Blog:
  http://musicindustryblog.wordpress.com/

  HypeBot:
  http://www.hypebot.com/

  Music 3.0:
  http://music3point0.blogspot.com/

  Dotted Music:
  http://dottedmusic.com/

- Note: this advice is current as of 2015. Things change. MXR will evolve. This book will get re-written. Meanwhile you will have placed your song, (provided it didn't suck).

- In the music business, all advice comes with an expiration date. Advice could be obsolete in 6 months. The world could go back to "I Left My Heart in San Francisco", or forward to a world where writing beats from a Geiger counter becomes the new hit thing.

- The order of all this may seem higgledy-piggledy, but imagine you and me sitting, talking, and discussing the situation. That's the idea of this book — a fireside chat!

- NOTE: From time to time you will see: **[****]** These are my semi-random observations, learned as a MIP reviewer of over 2000 incoming songs. I hope you'll find some of them useful.

- Actually, putting this document out into the world may be unwise on my part; because as you adopt these suggestions, the competition against my stuff will be that much keener.

II. ABOUT MUSIC XRAY & "THE FEES"

Why is MXR such a bonanza for writers?

- Mike McCready, the founder, is an honest broker. Over the years he nurtured MXR through several incarnations. New, unknown writers and artists now have a reliable conduit to real buyers, worldwide.

- Plus he's a nice, straightforward, likeable guy. He is what he says he is. You can watch several of his MXR backgrounder videos on YouTube, LinkedIn and MusicXray.com, and decide for yourself.

- MXR owns the "Big Ears". Meaningful, actual buyers of songs **use** MXR.

- The MXR "fee" system works. It balances the VERY FEW bona fide music buyers against UNCOUNTED MILLIONS of inundating songwriters.

- The serious buyers now see the advantages of having their inboxes "economically filtered". For the MIP, MXR is a major time saver.

- **About Music Xray & the "Fees".** You may disagree with the fee system. Other ways may exist to get your song to an A&R Exec at Universal Music Group. If you know one, by all means do your best. But with the few dollars of MXR fee, you're in a well-monitored, deliberate, straight line to genuine buyers. To me, it's a bargain at the price.

- And, much of the time, the fee goes to charity anyway. The fee is strictly a noise filter.

- The "Fee", (in quotes because the word "Fee" has such a negative connotation.) Think of it as "The-Cost-Of-Doing-Business", ("CODB"). To the poker playing writer, it's "The Ante".

  Some users call it: "Tuition-To-A-School-That-Teaches-Lessons-Unlearnable-Elsewhere."

  The naive writer views it as some kind of establishment rip-off, refuses to pay it, and refuses to avail himself of what MXR has to offer. And by "refusing", sadly closes some doors that most writers find very hard to open.

- The "CODB" has 3 parts:

  - A $10 "Diagnostics" Fee, (see Chapter XII for full details), payable ONCE PER SONG.

    You only **UPLOAD** your song **ONCE** - then you can submit it as often as you like.

   - A $5 "Submission" Fee payable ONCE PER SUBMISSION of a song to an opportunity.
   - In addition, the Listener/Buyer/MIP sets a "threshold" fee to discourage Tire-Kickers and Shotgun-Submitters. (Usually somewhere between $5.00 and $20.00).

- The logic:
   - The payback is a many times multiple of the threshold fee.
   - You believe in the song.
   - You're confident that you aren't wasting the MIP's time.
   - You demonstrate your confidence by paying the fee.
   - If you're not sure the song and the opportunity are just right for each other, then EVERYBODY is better off if you save your money.
- **Fees you NEVER pay at MXR**. You never pay a sign-up fee, or any monthly or annual "Dues". Everything is invested in the only thing that really matters: **The Song.**

[* * *] Look at it this way... The few dollars you pay is NOT to bribe the MIP into listening to your song --- but to SPARE the MIP from listening to all the "lame, noisy competition", (i.e. the songs you didn't write!)*

BTW - It has been known to happen that a writer uploads a song more than once by accident. If this happens, contact MXR and they will help cure the problem.

- How do you give your song the best shot? Let's look at the components:

    - Title
    - Audio
    - Lyric
    - Thumbnail Picture
    - Liner Notes
    - Comment ("Cover letter"), and
    - Timing of your submission ...

  ALL THESE THINGS MATTER. We compete with thousands of songs. Every tweak adds octane to the fuel.

As you will see ...

[* * *] NOTE: From time to time, I use the word "Guy". Such a person may be of any gender. "Guy" is simpler than "he or she" laced throughout the text.*

III. THE TITLE

"What's in a Name?" You ask?

- The Title holds 40% of the impact. The Title should pose a question that ONLY LISTENING TO THE SONG can explain.

  "Wrecking Ball", "Heartbreak Hotel", "Redneck Crazy", all make you want to know what the hell the song is ABOUT.

  Titles like: "I Can't Take The Chance", "Don't Leave Me", "Will We Ever Make It?", all tell you most of what you want to know before you ever click PLAY. Actually, ca 2015, one or two word titles are quite in fashion. Never make the title longer than the attention span of the audience you are writing for.

  A reviewer with a stack of ten songs will focus on the "compelling" titles first!

- Further, the Title MUST MATCH the song.

  The title must clearly evolve unambiguously from the song. Often, I've listened to songs wondering "What is going on here? THIS lyric is not about THIS title."

- Don't "explain" the title with a parenthetic subtitle. A little "cryptic" never hurt a title.

- Ask yourself: *Would this title fit any of a hundred different lyric plots equally well?* If so, start over. Is this title the one clear title the song could have? Songs that suggest more than one title confuse the listener's mind.

- "Roll Over Beethoven" can only be the title to ONE song. Ditto, "Hotel California" – these aren't skeleton key, one-size-fits-all titles. You can't write a song and then just name it something "appropriate". Bob Dylan could do this back when radio "named" the song for the listener. Nowadays, the song must name itself in the listener's mind.

- Whether you intend it or not, the mind titles the song by the first thing it hears repeated. Be sure the title ON the song matches the title IN the song.

- When using MXR, set the title, and only the title, wherever it appears, in **ALL CAPS**. Anywhere else, be very sparing in your use of ALL CAPS. Ideally, nothing but the title should be in ALL CAPS.

- BTW, for country songs, I'd avoid "funky" titles. Using "U" for "You", "Grl" for "Girl" etc.

- Remember: **THE TITLE IS THE BRAND.**

IV. THE LYRICS

The MUSIC gets the song into your head, but the LYRIC, is what keeps it there!

- ALWAYS POST THE LYRIC – ALWAYS – particularly if the demo is just a vocal with guitar or keyboard. The lyric doubles your odds of getting picked up in a search! ALWAYS POST THE LYRIC – ALWAYS.

- MXR's SEARCH feature scans the lyrics! The MIP who's looking for something special, will miss your song if its lyrics aren't in the database.

- MXR's method of inputting, editing and displaying lyrics is a little unintuitive, but it can be mastered.

- The best way to post the lyrics perfectly is to save them to a .TXT file; then copy the file into the lyric space. DON'T try to type them in. DON'T copy them from Microsoft Word in .DOC or .DOCX format. Importing from Word includes a bunch of hidden characters that may cause your lyrics to display garbled.

- Do not embed HTML. Don't jive anything, MXR's formatter discards most of it anyway. Leftover HTML fragments appear as garbled text. Always reduce your lyric to pure text (.TXT), then copy and paste it into place. (Use Microsoft's *Notepad* for the PC, or *TextEdit* for the Mac.)

- No BOLD FACE, No UNDERLINE, No ITALICS, especially No TABS. No Smiley Faces.

- Blank lines are OK, they're a MUST to make your lyric readable.

- Under the title, in parentheses, put the writers' names in caps and lower-case type. No more, no less. No "Lyrics by JOE", "Music by SALLY" etc., just one or two names:
  (Joe Blag – Sally Blog)

- Many times the lyric gets attention above and beyond the music itself. Make your presentation show you care.

- Proofread the lyric against the demo. Publish the lyric AS SUNG, not as written. If the singer changed a word or added a "just" or a "the", change the written lyric to match.

  There's a reason. The listener is eyeballing the lyric as he listens to the audio. If what he's reading and hearing fall out of sync, he immediately thinks: "Did I miss something?" "Why did the writer change it?" "The singer should know better than to *ad lib*." "Is this the wrong version?", and so on. The listener's main attention is interrupted. You can always touch up the lyric later – after the buyer expresses interest in the song.

- A perfectly formatted lyric is your best way to keep the listener focused on your song.

V. THE AUDIO

Where the rubber meets the road.

- Listeners form an initial impression in the first 20 seconds. Either:

    1. This Sucks.
    2. Who knows? I'll give it a little while.
    3. Some Talent here, let's hope they don't screw it up.
    4. "OMG what is this writer's phone number? I can't let this one get away!"

  I believe the final decision is made in the **first 45 seconds.**

  HENCE, starting a demo off with four measures of:

  STRUM, STRUM, STRUM, STRUM
  STRUM, STRUM, STRUM, STRUM
  STRUM, STRUM, STRUM, STRUM
  STRUM, STRUM, STRUM, STRUM

  ...drives the listener to madness. He thinks: "Here we go again." You've blown half the thermometer before you've sung a word.

Songs should arrest the listener's attention from the moment he hits PLAY. The first 20 seconds of the listener's attention is all you really *Own*. Don't blow it!

You aren't entitled to 3 minutes of undivided attention, if you can't compel 20 seconds of undivided attention.

Further to this, cue up your submission with no blank air at the start or the end of the song. When the listener clicks the PLAY button, you want your song in his face.

- Before you submit your song to MXR, be sure your demo is recorded at a good strong level. Not distorted, but comparable to what you hear on a current, hit, VEVO YouTube Video.

  Set your speaker playback level so the YouTube audio is comfortable, clear, and not faint. Then, without changing the settings, play your song. If your audio is faint in comparison, boost the level of your song as you record your .MP3 file, to get a good match.

  Once you post the song on MXR, PROOF-LISTEN TO THE SONG - END TO END. Something wrong? Fix it. Do this BEFORE you buy Diagnostics. Do this BEFORE you send the song to any MIP. If the track has flaws, delete it from MXR, then reload a fixed version.

(CHAPTER XII goes into detail about MXR's Diagnostics feature. Read this BEFORE you post your songs.)

- EDM records use long-mix-intros. However, your <u>demo</u> on MXR should cut to the chase and get to the good stuff. You can always make a dance record longer. But you want to sell the excitement up front. <u>In the liner notes, say an extended mix is available.</u>

- To me, demos of all kinds should END COLD – no fade outs. The reason is psychological and subtle. The MXR listener is not listening for enjoyment. He wants to DECIDE and go thumbs up or thumbs down.

  The long fade ending leaves him with the judgment call of "Heard enough? Anything new? I guess not, it's just fading, OK click." The cold ending says "OK Listener – let's go. Up, Down, or Replay it". You maintain some control over the situation.

- And LONG SOLOS waste your listener's precious attention. He can mentally interject an extended solo anywhere he pleases.

  Remember, the MIP thinks: "Including the video, I'm about to spend 100 Grand on this song. Is this THE ONE?" Ask yourself as you listen to your work: "If I were wrong and could lose my job, would I REALLY spend $100K on this song?"

- If a female is singing a demo of a song intended for a male, or vice-versa, the liner notes should say so clearly, otherwise the distracted reviewer must "figure it out".

- When you record a demo, listen to both a speaker mix and an earbud mix. Be sure the lyric is CLEAR in both cases. By speaker mix, I mean little cheap PC speakers, over which your song may be judged.

- Remember, for a DEMO, the lyric should be, above all else, understandable. The writer pitching a song is in a different game from an artist pitching a performance. Generally, in the MASTER of a performance, the lyric is mixed deeper into the mix; there's more going on in the track to mix the lyric into.

- Be careful about doubling the lead vocal on the VERSE of a demo. This can make the lyric muddy and difficult to understand. Doubling it on the chorus is OK, because the text is repeated, and the listener has more than one chance to identify what's being sung.

- Songwriters should remember – a demo is a demo and a master is a master.

  Sadly, most writers with limited resources use them to make their best attempt at a master. Spend wisely. Better you make a killer demo, than a limp master.

- The well-made DEMO deals only with a FIRM, CLEAR, SURE showcasing of the SONG. You are saying to the buyer: "Take this song and remake it from scratch with your artist."

- Artists face a different problem. You want to get "signed". You are saying, "Take ME, the performance, <u>and</u> the song. We both make money". The pitch must make this clear.

- In 2015 country songs, watch out for steel guitars, fiddles and banjos. Use them in a modern manner, not throwing back to the era of Bob Wills. *(I think MXR needs an "Americana" category, to hold country songs aimed at that legacy playlist. Meanwhile, make country demos for contemporary ears.)*

- The MXR technical staff says it can handle .MP3 files with any combination of compression factors and sample rates. If your software gives you a choice, use as little compression as possible.

- If you buy an expensive Nashville studio demo, always take away an instrumental track mix as well as the final vocal mix. If you re-think the lyrics later, you can experiment over the track, without going back to the studio for a costly, full re-do.

  "Store-bought" country demos can make your song sound much better than you can make it sound at home, but that doesn't make it a hit. A Nashville studio demo makes you feel good about your song, and your ego and family will feel you got your money's worth. BUT, this does not, in itself, make a hit.

[* * *] When your mother, wife, friend says: "Wow your song is GREAT!" What he/she is really saying is: "WOW that song is better than any song I could write!" – That's probably a true statement, but also far from guaranteeing a hit.*

BTW, you might look at 'REAPER', a digital audio workstation for PC or Mac. At $60 it gives you a lot of production/editing power for the money,

(http://www.reaper.fm/).

VI. THE THUMBNAIL PICTURE

"A picture is worth a thousand words." Here I think it's well worth the trouble...

- If you don't post a little Thumbnail picture, MXR puts up a gray box with the legend "No Image Available". This makes you look inept, or at the very least "not-up-to-speed".

- In 2015, no song becomes a hit without some kind of "visual". The image is your one frame, postage-stamp size music video!

- The MIP will click PLAY. You want him RIVETED to your pitch. His mind is being made up before you can take 3 deep breaths. His eye, *(and part of his mind)*, will tend to wander; give him a focus point.

  Do some Zen here. Give the listener SOMETHING to contemplate for the 3 minutes you're trying to own him.

- If the picture shows what this song is about, you've carved a tiny notch in his attention. You've boosted your cred.

[* * *] The MIP will probably receive your submission the instant you hit SEND. Most likely however, he will listen to songs in a batch. It's a "Task". As he clicks PLAY, he thinks: "Let this be the one! Let this be the one worth having listened to all the others. Let this not be a waste of time".*

- A well-chosen little picture shows the MIP: This writer knows what he's doing. It preps the MIP's expectation of quality, and gives him another cue to the workings of the song.

- Use an image big enough to convey something. Tight head shots beat full length. Graphics often work better than photos. Only use a picture of yourself if the part of you which shows is compelling.

- An inviting thumbnail ranks your submission in some slight way higher in the stack. The little picture says "Open Me First!"

- If the DEMO is SUNG by a woman, put up a picture of a woman.

- Use caution with a CD cover as a thumbnail picture. The image may be too tiny to clearly convey anything.

- A bunch of cuts from the album with the same picture blurs the focus of the pitch. Two different songs, two different images. Remember, it's a one-frame music video.

- The picture should be square. Not smaller than 200 pixels per side. Ideally 500 pixels square. All you need to manipulate images is a free program like GIMP, which is the poor-man's *Photoshop.* (www.gimp.org)

- Proofread the picture as it appears on MXR. If it comes out too small or strangely cropped, put up a different version. Your new version will automatically overwrite the old one. You can do this at any time.

[* * *] Photos: If you're a good-looking woman, put your head shot up, likewise a good-looking man. If "Mature", think twice. Paul McCartney can put his picture up, but he wouldn't if he weren't Paul McCartney Put up something. A logo maybe, not something irrelevant, and not an unappealing photo.*

VII. THE PRESENTATION

You don't need to "Game" the system, but you get best results if you "Use" it.

- Don't put an old date on a song you submit to MXR. If it's more than a year old, it will prejudice the listener, who will think: "Well if he couldn't sell it in 2012, why does he think I want it now?" It makes the song look like damaged goods.

- DO NOT APOLOGIZE FOR ANYTHING. If you feel you must apologize, save your money and don't put it up. Fix what you feel needs an apology, THEN put it up.

- *(Making this seamless is on MXR's docket of enhancements.)* When you submit, use the box provided for a NOTE to the MIP who will be evaluating your music. **You need to make clear, in the message to the MIP, exactly what you're selling.**

  Set the Reviewer's focus with something like:

  - "This is a Demo. I'm a writer trying to get this song recut by another artist."
  - "We're a group, looking to get signed; rate

the whole package, song + performance."

- "I'm an artist/writer. Ideally I'd like to be signed as an artist, but if you'd like to use the song but not my performance, that's OK." *(To me, this is the WORST strategy.)*

  If you intend to do this, better you should first make your pitches to the Buyers of You- as-an-artist. Give it a few months. If that fails, "detach" this song from your career as an artist, and pitch the song itself.

- "These are instrumental MUSIC CUES, designed for sync to a soundtrack."
- "I own all rights to this song and seek to license it for sync to a film soundtrack."
- "This is a 'Cabaret' song or special material designed for live performance."
- "This is EDM designed for DJ use, and for the dance charts."
- "This is a *rough sketch* of a song for feedback, to determine if I should develop or abandon the idea."
- "This is a remix of an existing recording as a sample of my skill as a remixer."
- "This is a mixed instrumental BED/BEAT awaiting a top-line vocal."

    - Cover Versions: Frankly, I think this is fertile ground, but you must use care in your presentation.

      "This is a cover version of 'X' written by 'Y & Z', published by 'ABCD' who own the copyright in the underlying work. We *(meaning you the performer)* claim copyright only in this recorded performance of the work."

- A lot of auto-bio stuff is potentially more un-selling than selling. Let the song, the title, and the lyric make the sale. It is said: "More sales were killed by the jawbone of an ass than any other weapon." Less blather is more.

- If you're offshore to the USA, I think you <u>should</u> make this known as part of your pitch. American ears perk up to the possibility of the next "PSY" or "Lorde"

- When you're pitching a <u>song</u> and not you as an artist, maybe don't list it as part of an album. It might be seen as a "used" song, recycled merch.

- <u>The reviewer's mind-set:</u> In the "old days" the reviewer faced a bushel basket filled with crumply manila envelopes and FedEx packages, each containing a cassette, leaking the hopes and dreams of the aspiring writer.

The reviewer set out to work his way through the stack. Twas a task, because the ratio of good stuff to mediocre stuff was tiny. Maybe one good usable song out of 50 listens.

Flash: Now online, it's much the same, (Though I realize you wrote "the one" while the other guys wrote the other 49.)

- For the TITLE, enter only the TITLE, no quotes, no strange characters, no author's name, just the title, in ALL CAPS.

- After you see your package in MXR's format, edit it until it's clear and uncluttered. Rinse & repeat until perfect.

- MXR gives you three choices for a genre. Pick exactly ONE, the closest target. If rejected, change genres for the next pitch. Don't try to be all things to all people. No one song is perfect for *Electronica, Soul,* and *Country*. Show the listener you respect his niche.

- When choosing your genre, don't select "Unclassifiable". It shows weakness.

- You have two places to post a note or comment about your song:

    1. The "Liner Notes" – linked to the audio and the lyric. All viewers of the song see the liner notes.

2. The private message to the MIP – entered at the time you submit your song to a dropbox. It's seen only by the MIP.

Think about what you are writing. You can edit the liner notes later, but you can't un-send the private message.

Whatever you say is unlikely to cause the MIP to "buy" the song which doesn't sell itself. The MIP will make the first contact with you via MXR. Then you and the MIP will be "chatting" and you can say what you like.

MXR gives your pitch about 8 square inches of screen real estate. The buyer doesn't care – at this point – about anything concerned with your life and career. That comes later, when the buyer wants to buy what he hears.

- The object is to post a little something in the liner notes and private message, so you look like you care; but not to post anything that makes you look like a dip.

- Never make unsubstantiated claims! (*"I'm the best lyric writer in Iowa"* – which may in fact be true, but it's unprovable.)

- You even need to watch substantiated claims: *"I won the 2007 NSAI Award."* Which may be true but so what? How does that affect what the MIP is listening to now?

- Now, if in 2015 you can say "I won the 2014 award", that's current and may make sense. (As I said elsewhere, use caution putting dates on a submission unless it is the current year. Likewise, don't refer to things in the commentary which date the song.)

- Nothing in the name of the group, the artist, the website, the lyric, typos, flaws in the mix -- nothing -- should cause the reviewer the slightest negative thought. Proofread/Proof-listen to what you're sure is already perfect; you probably missed something.

- If your material is country, be sure your User Name and email address don't sound totally "sci-fi", or "punk-rock". Give the MIP the feeling he is dealing with somebody sane. Somebody he would invite into his office.

- Don't hawk that you've written hundreds of songs. Most likely, most of them suck.

- Don't set your MyBandSite to play automatically when you hit the landing page. *(Some think this intrusive web design is tacky.)*

  Because, if the MIP clicks "MyBandSite" to check out your website while he's listening to your song, the two soundtracks will collide in a scrambled cacophony

MyBandSite will sway borderline ratings in the negative direction if the site looks weird or fails to open.

- Further, AFTER you put a link to MyBand-Site or FaceBook or SoundCloud or YouTube... Click on each of these links to be sure that:
  - The link actually works perfectly
  - The linked content enhances your case.

  If the link is broken, don't submit the song to a dropbox till you fix the link.

- NOTE: Proof-linking is YOUR responsibility, not MXR's - but they will certainly work with you to de-bug any link problems you have.

- Pitching Instrumental sound cues for film/ video background: This is tough. Currently MXR has no good way to classify the demo as a sound cue. There's a steady demand for sound cues and quick-turnaround writers...

  So your demo must generate a desire in the listener to get in touch with you, based on his assessment of your TALENT, more than his assessment of one particular submission.

  Were I a Cue Composer, I'd make a package called "3 Cues Terror" or "5 Cues Romance" with 20 or 30 second "stings" separated by spaces. *(Naturally I would avoid a package named "4 Cues.")*

[****] And about "The Presentation", follow this. It's true. In the cassette days, I used to make this bet and win every time. ...

Assume 2 cassettes arrive in the mail:

- *Writer A's tape contains one song.*
- *Writer B's tape contains six songs.*

Looking for a "hit", you'd think the odds favor Writer B, six to one. ... WRONG!

Given only the above information, you know, without ever opening either bag, the hit is more likely to be in Bag A.

Can you figure out the inexorable reason why?

BECAUSE: If a writer, who wants to sell songs to artists were good enough to write a hit, he would clearly know that he had written it. HENCE, once he had written it, he would not waste time writing 5 more songs before showing it around – he would lick the stamp and send it.

AND he would know not to dilute the impact of the potential hit with 5 other items which might un-sell the buyer.

- As a writer, think twice about putting a link to *CDbaby*. You're not SELLING a CD to the listener for $10.00; you want him to invest $$$ in your song! If he contacts you for more info, send him a free CD by FedEx.

- To suppress the legend "No Album name set", and leave the album title completely empty, enter three blank spaces.

- If your song is weak, submit it on a slow day. Submit a strong song on a busy day. (There's a good reason.) Busy days occur a couple of times a month when MXR runs "two-fer" specials. Using the offer, many writers will "experiment" with songs – maybe not the top of their output – thinking "What the heck, I'm paying for the submission of the important song, maybe I'll get lucky with the other one." Thus, the competition on the busy days, falls way off, and a strong song looks terrific.

- VITAL – The first time you present a song, do all your uploading and editing of the song presentation BEFORE you select a MIP's dropbox. With the dropbox link open while you're editing the lyric, you could accidentally hit "SEND" and mail a garbled copy. SOLIDIFY the package first – get the Diagnostics, THEN troll for opportunities.

- In your liner notes, don't describe what the song '*is*' (or what you think the song '*says*'). The listener should be evaluating the song – not determining whether his evaluation compares with your evaluation!

- When you buy diagnostics, MXR looks at the Genre(s) you specified. It then sends your song to five randomly selected MIPs with expertise in that genre, who will listen and provide the initial ratings.

- On "Two-Fer" days, you can post two songs for the price of one and save $10.00. You want to spread the songs across the greatest number of ears. Submit to two different genres. e.g., Song "A" to "POP" and Song "B" to "Country". To encourage randomness, put them up one at a time, with a few hours between submissions.

Generally, don't submit two songs to a MIP at the same time. If he passes on one, it may impact his decision on the other.

- The MIP has a stack to go through. He usually starts with an open mind. But after hearing 5 or 6 "weak" songs, his patience for weakness grows thin, and you may receive a less than charitable rating.

  That said, you don't want "charitable" ratings. You get those from your wife and mother. IF your song is weak – while it may sound better than other weak songs – it won't hold up against the one or two really great songs the MIP hears in a week of listening.

- The whole package must make the listener feel that lurking in here somewhere is:

  1. A song I can use, or
  2. A writer who could fix any flaws in it.

  Or better still,

  3. A writer with enough talent to write me a new song on demand. Let's call him up!

  All other conclusions lead the MIP to silently mutter, *Sorry – Next Case – Click.*

To summarize: whatever you put up on MXR – visual, verbal, musical, promo - whatever you put up there - must convey:

- Solidity
- Assuredness
- Confidence. Not Bravado! Not Smoke-Blow. Not A-Lick-and-A-Promise, but the feeling that you and the song are strong. That it is, and you are, THE REAL DEAL.

VIII. BUSINESS & MXR

Put yourself in the mind of the person who's considering your song.

- You hear stories: *"I showed this song to 30 publishers. I was rejected by them all. Then Number 31 picked it up. The rest is history!"* In all probability, the version publisher 31 heard was NOT the same version the first 30 rejected!

- Prepare to abandon weak stuff and improve stuff with potential. I know of no shopped around song that was not touched up somehow between the demo and the sale.

- *"What Are You Looking For?"* You ask? All buyers give you the same answer: *"I can't tell you what I want, but I'll know it when I hear it… but I can easily tell you what I don't want the minute I hear it."*

- Remember too, the listener is NOT in the opinion or coaching business. Sad but true. His obligation – as they would say in Congress – is an Up or Down vote on whether or not he can use the song he's hearing. **SOMETIMES**, you do get feedback or an encouraging note from the MIP, particularly where your song is a "near-miss" for some reason or other. This is a bonus.

- MXR does offer presentations from Coaches/ Editors who will, for a fee, try to help you fix what's weak. These MIPs clearly identify themselves as consultants – not buyers of songs. This may be just what you need.

- With MXR, you try to match what you've got with what the buyer claims to want. If you're a quick-turnaround writer with a home studio, it might make more sense to WRITE SOMETHING THAT FITS FROM SCRATCH, rather than "shoehorn" a song from your trunk into the opportunity.

- We must all be reminded, the listener is rejecting the SONG, not rejecting YOU the PERSON. Move On. Next Case.

- I feel MXR is an honest broker – The MIPs are not shills. They are square-business. MXR does its best to research the *bona fides* of potential MIPs. They police the system and 'off' the rare MIP who turns out to be a shill.

- MXR is trying to walk the straight path between the writers who desperately need the listeners, and the listeners who DON'T need the traffic from thousands of writers, but who DO need a useful song.

- MXR attempts to change what the buyers see as a needle in a haystack, into A HAYSTACK BUILT OF NEEDLES.

- See Sturgeon's Law: "90% of everything is Crap." That includes my songs, your songs, AND the records a label releases from the songs they actually DO buy. That's a fact of life and must be lived with.

- So use your judgment, but it may be best to remove continually rejected songs from MXR. If you tweak a listener's interest with something he likes, you don't want to un-tweak it by his hearing other, "weaker" songs in your catalog

  If you put a song up, and want to revise it, you have two choices:

  1. Take the original song down and replace it with the new version
  2. Leave the original in place and put up a clearly MARKED "VERSION 2", and edit the title of the original to show it as "VERSION 1".

Either course of action will cost you the $10 Diagnostics fee. *(See Chapter XII on Diagnostics.)* But replacing the original will wipe out the song's earlier Diagnostics, Fans and Submissions, and it will no longer be visible to MXR searches.

Putting up two versions allows a coach access to both of them for comparison. Two versions could confuse, if not clearly labeled.

- Be concerned if you are linking to entire albums on SoundCloud. You may be exposing a mix of your good stuff diluted with "filler".

- MXR says there's no restriction on submitting the same song twice to the same MIP. This is both a *Feature* and a *Bug*.

    - *Feature*: If you feel strongly about your song you can pay the fee again, ramp up the cover letter and resubmit it. Nothing in the technology prevents you from a double dip. Nothing encourages you to do it either. However it is doable.

    - *Bug*: You could accidentally double click and double submit and thereby double bill your PayPal. If this happens, contact MXR, they will make all necessary adjustments, no problem.

    It's up to you to keep track of your submissions, and not accidentally send the same one twice to the same MIP. (See the *Submission Management feature of MXR in Chapter XII.*)

- Read 25 archived issues of Lefsetz; then go back over your catalog. If you're too discouraged to continue writing as you do now, you've done yourself a favor. You'll either:

quit to pursue something more rewarding, get a new collaborator, or take a break and clear your head.

- That said, "Taking a break to clear your head", will not get the songs written or sold. So get back to work.

- If rejection's a problem for your ego, submit under a "Pen Name". No problem. MXR allows you multiple identities, but each needs its own unique email address.

- Re: *Pen Names*, **everybody should do this**, just to own some private piece of the internet. Create a brand new Google-proof first and last name. Make it so unique that a search on it comes up empty. Immediately register the Dot-Com of the name, (about $10.00 at GoDaddy). Get the Gmail address too. Keep this name in inventory. The time will come when the effort will pay off. A Google-unique name is the best gift you can give an artist, writer, or your next kid.

- If you DO get a nibble from a buyer, don't immediately glom or swamp him with more stuff. Stick to one basic sale. One song. Stay focused. Get one song done first.

- Remember, once the guy has picked your song, he really, really wants it, because it's so much better than the 200 he's rejected.

Keep this in mind when the time comes to negotiate your deal with the buyer.

- The buyer for a label doesn't want music that *sounds like* what's currently on the air. He wants a writer who knows everything that is now, or ever was, on the air, who has created something new and commanding.

- However, the buyer who wants to license a song for a particular film scene, often DOES want something familiar sounding.

  Buyers will list or load reference songs to MXR that suggest the feel they seek. These listings guide your selection of a likely fit from your catalog.

  Also, MXR's software matches the loaded songs against its song database which contains your material. MXR sends you an email if a matching run turns up one of your songs that fills the need.

  Often, a film producer will use a popular but pricey track as a rough work background during editing. The music supervisor must then find similar, but lower cost, material. Listen to the reference samples, if your song is in the same bag, it could wind up in a film.

- MXR is not a mutual admiration society for writers. It's a pipeline. A "Yes or No".

But, to interact with other writers and trade insights, you might want to sign up as an MXR Fan and listen to submissions by your contemporaries. *(In the next edition of MXR, Fans will be able to provide feedback to the writers of songs they like.)*

For an Artist/Writer, listening as a Fan to other MXR writers' work is very educational. Listen to 25 songs. You'll hear a mixed bag. Judge the IMPACT of these 25. By "IMPACT", I mean the total of the song's music, lyrics, demo, and spiel. How the song "hits" you.

You need to ask yourself: *"Is my best presentation at least as good as the best of these 25?"* If so, you've probably got a good shot. If not, maybe some polish is in order.

[* * *] MXR has a hidden agenda – Namely as presentations, songs, and writers thereof, get better, stronger, and more "in touch", the MIPs easily get what they want. In an uncluttered world, MIPs will preach the efficacy of MXR around the water-cooler of the music industry.*

[* * *] The nice part about MXR; once you and the MIP forge a communication link and mutual respect, you've got an important new contact, and MXR is out of the loop.*

[* * *] Oh... And technically, MXR sometimes has problems with AOL. (Probably more accurately put: AOL has problems.) If you use AOL for email etc., use Chrome or some other browser when you interact directly with MXR.*

IX. SONG CONSTRUCTION

(Maybe this book is a little bit about "How to write a song"... A few thoughts.)

- In country songs, it's OK to drink if you're having a good time; but a song about a depressed drinker is a hard sell.

- Beware the "Lyric Writer's Melody" (especially in country). It is composed by someone who writes pretty good lyrics but has no strong composer to collaborate with. Such melodies tend to "hover" and go nowhere. Cure this with an assertive collaborator.

  The song with a mediocre lyric written by a killer composer will generally fly. One with a lame melody written by an arch lyricist rarely gets off the ground. *(Trust me on this one!)*

- Electronica: As software to make loops or beats is available to any geek with an iPad, many geeks with iPads will try it.

  It's much easier to make a passable dance track than an equivalent rock or country song; but in the marketplace, the Electronica bar is just as high as the Pop bar.

Don't dash off Electronica with the idea... "Isn't it neat how the software does all the work?" You are competing against producers with lifetimes of EDM experience.

Thought, craft, construction, variety, development and progression is required for <u>any</u> song you want heard all the way through – more than once. Especially EDM.

- Dance Electronica stands a better shot if it has SOME verbal content. Even non-semantic (meaningless) melisma. The voice is a vital component of the crowd experience.

- Further: IF your Electronica has a new, strong vocal/verbal/sonic texture, sneak peek it into the first minute, otherwise it won't get heard if the bored listener clicks out.

- Re "Chill Music" – Electronica: Until MXR makes a separate category for this, it's a tough sell. You're more likely to get noticed by writing something "up" and energetic.

- Be very wary of lyrics which flip the logic of the song 3/4 of the way through with "BUT":

    - The lyric starts out: *"It isn't. It's not, I won't. You won't. We won't."* etc.
    - <u>BUT</u> for some Blah-Blah-Blah reason, disregard everything!
    - NOW *"It is, I will, and we will!"*.

This kind of structure was popular in earlier eras, but now can sound difficult. In a click-easy world, following a lyric with a lot of "logic" is asking too much of many listeners.

- The lyric can't be convoluted, swiveling back on itself. The plot, if there is one, must be CLEAR. Not flipping amongst a bunch of "IF… Maybe…But... Before… Then... After…" constructs. What could be clearer than: "*I met him on a Monday and Da Do Ron Ron*"?

- Reality and the song lyric: You can't use unalloyed reality as the stuff of a song. Start with reality if you must, but dump it when fiction and invention make a stronger work.

  I once had a guy in class who wrote a killer, killer love song. He called it "*Phyllis*" – I asked, "Why in hell did you call it '*Phyllis*'"? – He said "'Cause that's her name."

  When you are standing at the corner of Art and Truth – Turn right and head down ART.

- In intense songs where the lyric is the focus, 3 words to avoid: "Just", "But" and "Autopsy". Avoid tentative words like "maybe", "hope", "wonder", "think".

- Avoid drizzly verb forms like: "have had", "could it be". Avoid words that only exist in the head.

- Use nouns you can **SEE,** verbs where something **HAPPENS**. "Wrecking Ball" – you can visualize in action even if you've never heard the song.

- All this said... The lyric of the modern, pop, 200 million view, YouTube hit, is often a cocktail of very simple words, many repeated, many times, chunked into a mosaic; intermingled with a few semi-surreal words to snag the "pop listener's" recollection, and to give the video designer something to hang the sequence on. (...**And a Killer Title!**)

- BALLADS - Generally only established artists can release a sad ballad. MIPs and the public want up-tempo, engaging, positive stuff. New artists (the kind the new writer is most likely to connect with), generally get their start with UP material. Pitching downers and ballads is a harder row to hoe.

- Every now and then, write a love lyric without using the word "Love". Imagine yourself as a creative photo journalist covering a basketball game; shoot 100 pictures without including an image of the basket.

- Beware ballads where you telegraph the rhyme to the listener. You've heard the song which goes: "blah-blah-blah PAIN" and you know the next line will be "blah-blah-blah … RAIN". At slow tempos, your lines must be especially engaging, because the listener has time to LISTEN to them!

- That's the nice part about RAP; the pace is so fast, the listener can't out-think the writer.

- Attend to prosody. What is "prosody" you ask? It is the FIT between the words and the tune. It's why the phrase "Ole Man River" sounds wonderful and "No More Tuesday" sounds awful to the same melody.

- Good prosody means you don't shoehorn words into songs, where the accents of the words as sung must be jimmied to fit the scansion of the melody. The listener thinks: "amateur", "not ready for prime time".

- The song must PAY OFF. Somewhere you must get the message: *This is where the song was going from the first thump. Ahh... this explains it. This is neat. This is Wow.* Homogeneous, soupy lyrics, and wishy-washy songs won't show up on the radar. Spend your time **Perfecting The Outrageous**.

- A writer can't "fake" a country song. Genuine country people write genuine country hits. You can't interlope. Don't think dropping a lot of dogs, trailers and brand names into your lyric will make it "country".

- The lyric to a *country* song must make sense, not be just a bunch of phrases which sometimes rhyme.

- Interestingly, in a country song, whenever someone is in a car going TO someplace, they're always RETURNING TO a specific happy place, (*honky-tonk on the corner, grandma's farm, etc.*) When driving AWAY FROM someplace, they're heading for parts TOTALLY UNKNOWN.

- With female country lyrics: The protagonist – the woman the song's about – can't cast an image that reflect's badly on the singer herself. She can't sing "I'm weak, I'm pitiful, I can't cope.", and then expect the audience to want her autograph after the show.

- The hit song says what the listener has never heard aloud before, but has had inside him always. Hits are writ in the DNA.

- Just as it's hard for a band to get traction, exposure, "likes", and an audience, it's harder than ever for a writer to get a song cut by another artist.

  For a writer in 2015, your probable best shot is pure, up-tempo, right down the middle POP; or if you can write a real one, a country song. Certainly somewhere out there is another titanic Carole King, Brian Wilson,

Billy Joel, or John Lennon, who will come along and grab EVERYBODY. A writer/performer who towers over the music scene.

Meanwhile, if you're not fortunate enough to be that person - you need to hook up to artists who have a public and need killer material. Right now, (2015) it seems straight ahead broadcast radio Pop, EDM, or contemporary Country, is your best entryway.

That said - always err on the side of outrage rather than milk-toast. The MIP who doesn't like the milk-toast song generally doesn't **recall it or it's writer**. Many times a disliked "challenging" song causes the MIP to take note of who wrote it ... **for the future**.

The writer's Klondike: Seek a talented new artist who is a great performer but who can't write a lick. This is the ideal find.

- Looking over the hundreds of dropboxes opened by MIPs looking for material, the CLEAR TREND is towards fully finished, ready-to-broadcast "masters". This is understandable because:
    - Competition is dense now. The MIP has a broad range of tunes from which to select.

      When it's a toss-up between two songs, the nod often goes to the slicker sounding package. The MIP's specs will request:

"Master quality only" or "Demos OK". This is usually a pretty strict criterion.

Don't expect a scruffy production, of even a great song, to get you across, when the MIP wants broadcast-ready submissions. This is just a fact of life.

- Competition's tougher too, because inexpensive desktop software lets the talented musician make a broadcast-ready production right at home. Thus the overall cut-off for what is "acceptable" has gone way up over the standards of ten years ago.
- The "pitcher/plugger" is looking to make a quick, direct, niche-sale, to move a specific song into a specific, immediate need.

  Versus the traditional, full-line publisher, who views himself as a spotter of promising songs which he can enhance with full blown demos, and promote to a wide market over a long period of time.

  The plugger ideally wants material in a ready-to-sell-right-now finished format, with no additional re-recording required.

For all these reasons – the bar is now a high one. But it's equally high for everybody.

X. GLOSSARY

Disclaimer: Neither the author of this book, MXR, nor any specific person at MXR is offering or purporting to offer any legal advice or counsel. You have the obligation to secure such advice for yourself from your own legal advisor.

NOTE: Some MIPs play different roles with different opportunities. If a MIP shows interest in your song, make sure your relationship is clear.

Glossary of MXR "Roles": MXR MIPs fall roughly into these categories:

1. **An End User of the song:** A buyer. A person with the authority to green-light a recording of your song on their label – either with you as the artist, or with an artist in their stable.

2. **A Pitcher/Plugger:** A middleman. A person with an address book of good, high-level, song-buying contacts. How to compensate such a middleman is the question:

- A finder's fee from the buyer
- A flat fee from you
- A percentage of the income he generates
- A piece of the song's publishing income
- All of the song's publishing income.

The pitcher/plugger is not an end user. He is only as valuable as the artists he has direct access to. The song must do the work once the plugger gets it in the door.

The plugger has his credibility at stake with each pitch. He only sees an open door, when he's known for pitching "good stuff". Weak material is too risky.

Ideally you need an agreement with "re-capture rights", so if the plugger can't produce, you'll retain/recapture all the rights in your song. You will need these rights to get the song cut elsewhere.

3. **The true Music Publisher:** A company who wants to "Sign your song", sometimes with an advance, most often not. The publisher's job is to promote the song to artists, films, TV and all other markets, domestic and foreign.

   The publisher will collect mechanical royalties and licensing fees from users and remit a portion to you. In a typical deal, the publisher (or the group of publishers if there is more than one involved), will keep 50 cents of every dollar the song takes in – normally in perpetuity.

   The publishing company may be huge "*Universal Music Group*" or small "*Plibby*". In either case, the company would, should, could, use its best efforts to get the song exposed worldwide.

Theoretically, once the song is published, you no longer need to work the tune. In reality, to squeeze the most juice from your catalog, working your own songs, published or not, is a lifetime occupation.

Be aware that many publishing companies are merely file drawers. They are the Sargasso Sea of lost copyrights. Be sure when you sign your song to a publishing company, that you are signing to a person who can do you some genuine good.

(Also note, as a writer, you are entitled to the writer's share of performance royalties that flow to you directly, around the publisher, via ASCAP, BMI or SESAC... But that's another book entirely.)

4. **The Coach:** For a fee, the coach critiques your song, giving you advice on how to improve it. *(In this book, you just bought much of what I'd say if you had me do a critique of your song. I genuinely hope you find value here.)*

   Coaching is valuable if it is critically meaningful. Especially if the coach is honest enough to tell you to "shelve" a song, that the salvage work would be better spent on something new. You don't want "comfort", you want coaching.

Some coaches with contacts can steer you to possible buyers. Some coaches do plugging for a fee. Thus, you need to be clear on your exact relationship with a coach.

5. **The Music Supervisor:** Works for a Film/TV/Advertising Agency, either as an employee or a free-lancer. He must find SPECIFIC music, for specific needs – usually right now, or on a 1 to 6 months horizon. He needs what he needs; anything else is a waste of everybody's time.

   Many opportunities exist for licensing to budget films and made-for-TV movies. Fees are correspondingly modest, but there is a lot of traffic here. It's a good way for a new writer to get on the scoreboard.

   The "sync" license is for a specific use where the music is locked to a motion picture. The music supervisor is not (generally) asking for ownership of the song, just the right to use it in a specific situation.

   WARNING - Clearance is vital. Every performer and collaborator must grant written permission to use his contribution. SAMPLES: Do not present a song containing samples unless you absolutely know what you are doing! You will need lawyerly guidance.

6. **The Licensing firm:** The music supervisor, who is often harried, with many items on his plate, will ask a licensing firm to: *"Get me some Fiesta Music," "I need a song about a Rainbow,"* etc. The licensing firm tries to connect the dots, with you as one dot, the music supervisor as the other. The same lawyerly advice applies here too.

7. **The Library:** This is a licensing firm that builds a catalog in advance of demand. They expect to be asked *someday* to supply "a song about a rainbow". They will add your rainbow song to their library.

   Then *someday*, a music supervisor will call that firm on the assumption its library has thousands of songs, including one about a rainbow. This placement will generate a license with payment split between the library and the writer.

   This idea works well for writers who own their own publishing. They can list the song non-exclusively with several libraries, or list only the licensing rights to one library exclusively.

   NOTE: There is risk to a non-exclusive license of a "race to the bottom", where two different libraries are competing to get your song placed in the same slot. This exclusive vs. non-exclusive question, needs a thorough investigation to get the ideal arrangement. Do your homework here. You might be better off parking your catalog exclusively in an aggressive far reaching library, than non-exclusively in a bunch of "passive" libraries, but both sides of the argument have merit.

If you are a quick-turnaround composer of cue music, an aggressive library is a good long-term place to be. If MXR gets you in the door, your Fees were well spent!

Some libraries offer a flat, one-time-payment, all-rights, buy-out of the song. With this option there would be no subsequent earning from the song. There's nothing *a priori* wrong with this, just be sure you are clear on the terms of your deal.

8. **Internet Radio Stations & Podcasts:** Generally no harm done here. Internet radio is in some sense a "vanity press" for the performing artist, but *Hey, you never know.* Your song might get heard in places near and far, by listeners who want to hear stuff they can't get on terrestrial radio. As an artist, you could get picked up, blogged and booked by somebody who loves your material.

XI. NEW SONG SET-UP

Here's how to get your song into the system.

1. Log In - Go to www.musicxray.com - You'll see this screen:

2. After you Log In (or get signed-up as a first time user,) you will see:

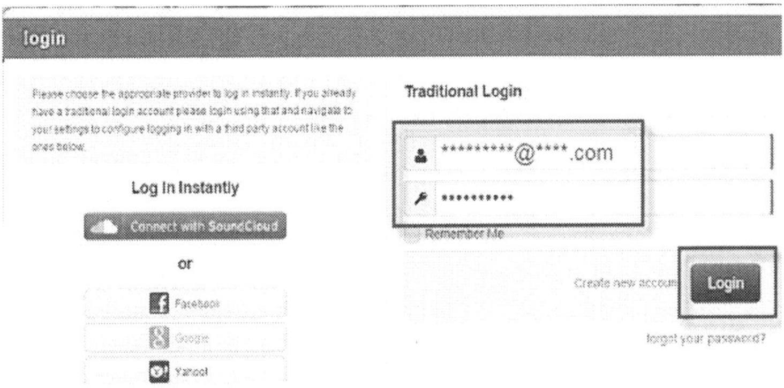

3. Get the track exactly as you want it. Use .MP3 Format. Use a hot but undistorted level. Lyrics clear in the mix. No dead air at the start or end of the song. Upload it to MXR.

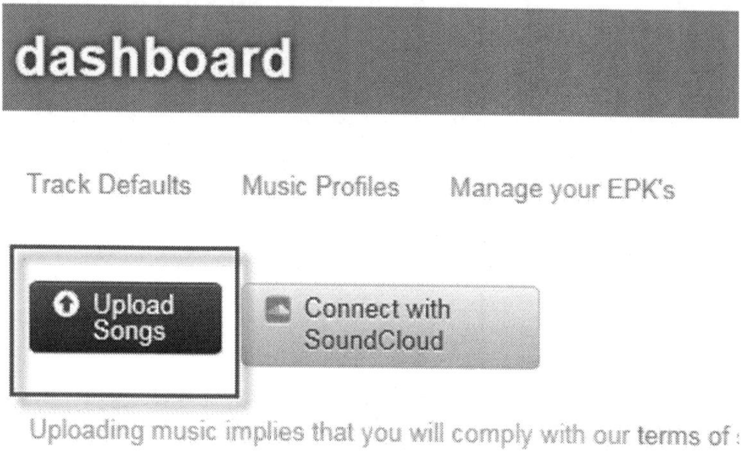

4. As you click "UpLoad Songs", you'll see a File Dialog Box. Select the .MP3 you want to upload.

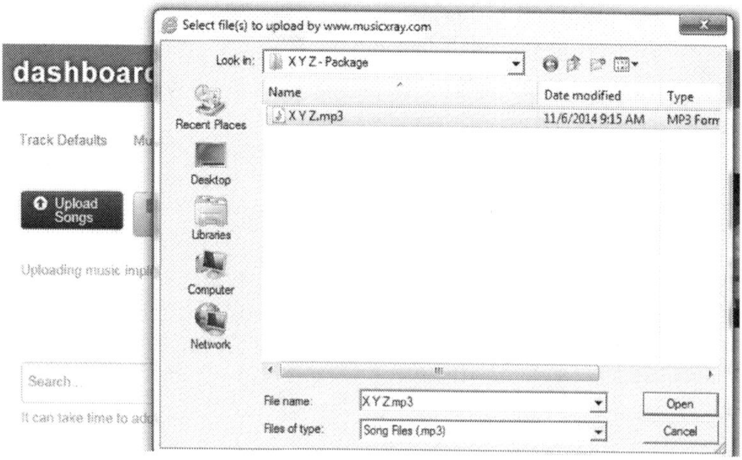

5. When the upload is complete, your song will appear at the top of your list of titles.

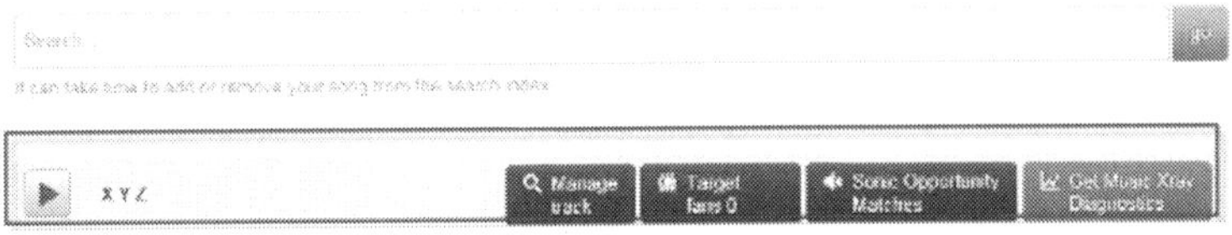

6. **Don't Order Diagnostics yet**, you have more to do first.

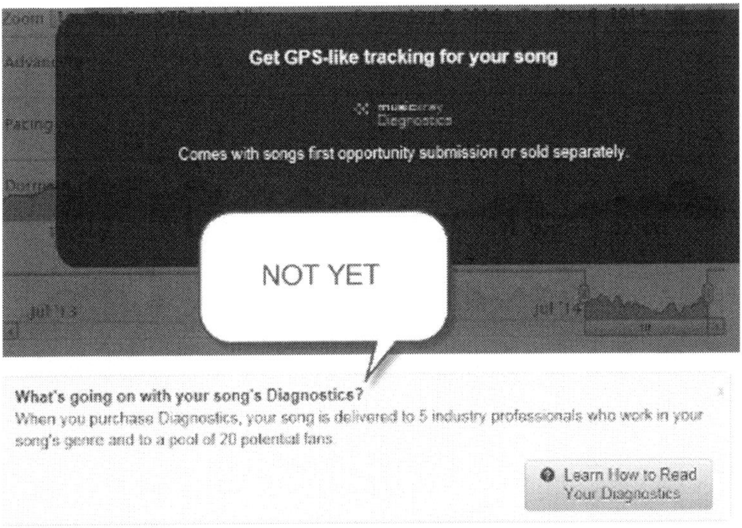

7. Now go to EDIT SONG

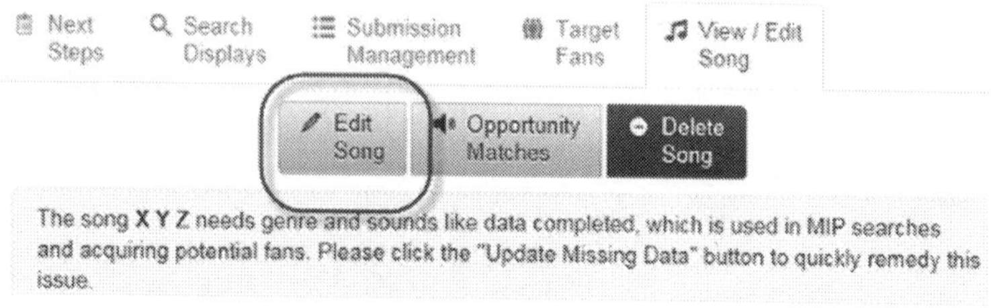

8. Enter the Facts. Title. Album Name (OR 3 Blank spaces if there is no album name), and the Artist Name.

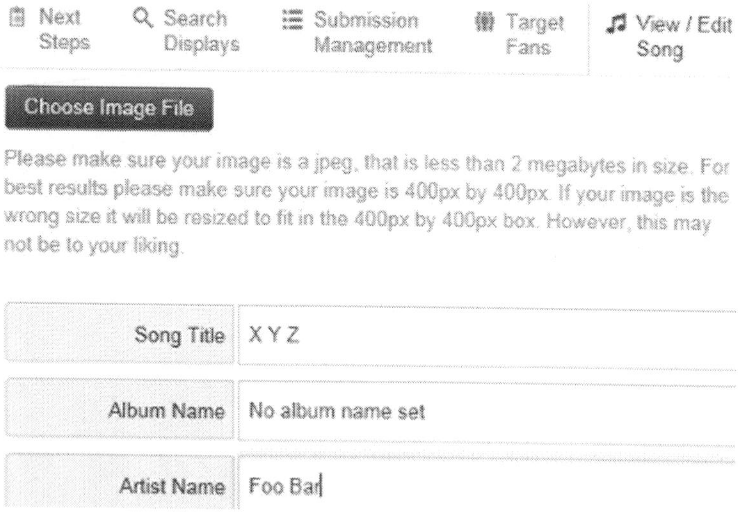

9. Add the YEAR - ideally the current year or no year. Pick a GENRE. (You can pick 3 but use care, don't blur the focus.) If you are downloading from SoundCloud, you'll need to add: Track number, Total Tracks, and Disc Number.

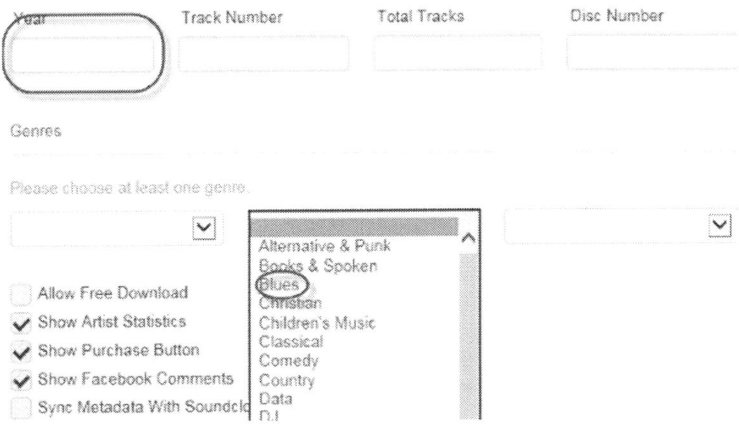

10. Fill in these boxes: **Especially the lyrics**.

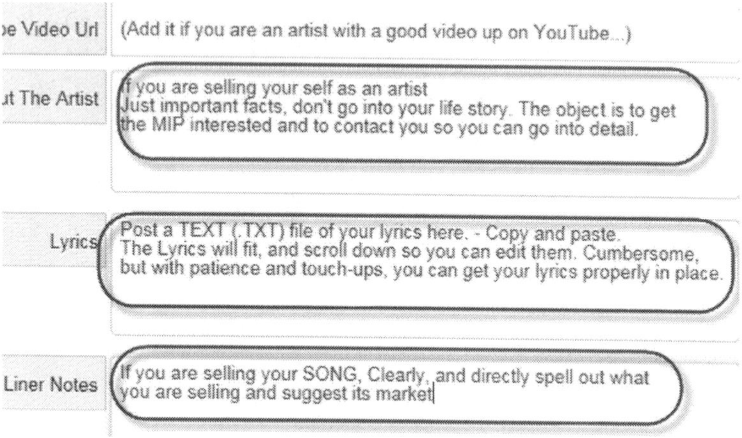

11. When in doubt. Select "All Rights Reserved." AND in the License Contact Info Box put PHONE, address, and Email address.

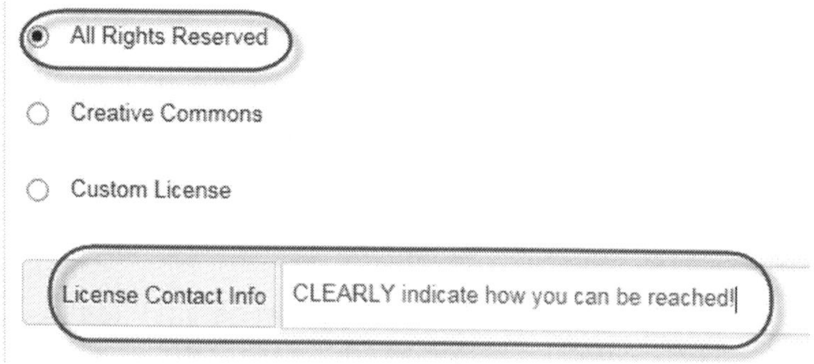

12. Add a MOOD. This aids MIPs who are searching for a specific situation e.g., a film.

If the song only fits a male or a female, select that in the FEATURED VOCAL. If anybody can sing it, leave this field BLANK.

BPM (Beats Per Minute) will give a user of EDM an idea of your song's tempo. For ballads and most other songs, this is not so important, but it never hurts to add it. If you don't add any of these values you are not "penalized", but you should take a minute to complete these fields.

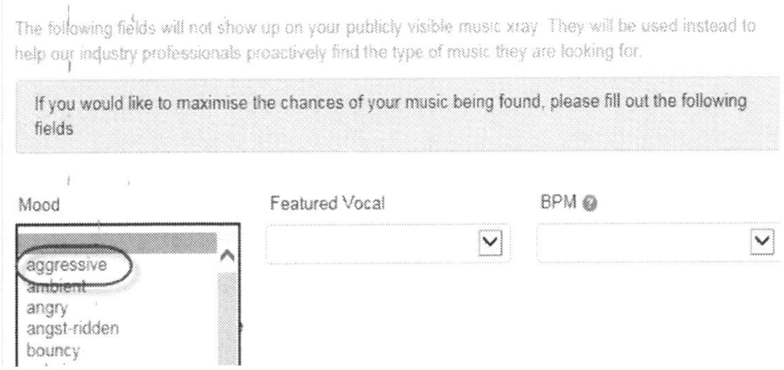

13. To get feedback from Fans, enter the names of THREE artists you think represent the feel of your song. Your song will be sent to 20 fans of those artists. This should give a representative fit and an honest indication of how your song stacks up to a listener who enjoys your TYPE of music.

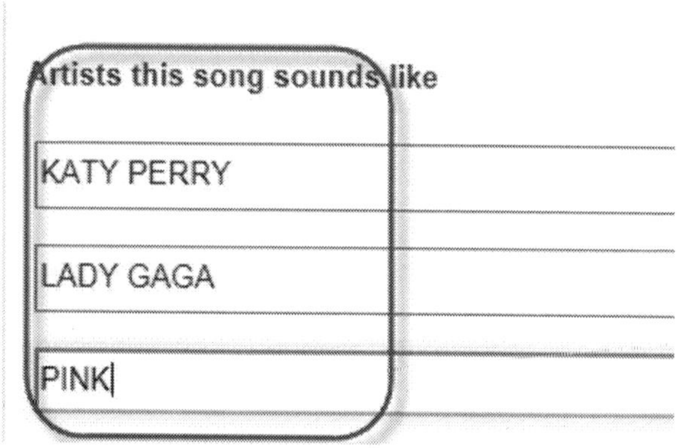

14. Hit SAVE - to set the song up on MXR.

15. Your work will now look something like this...

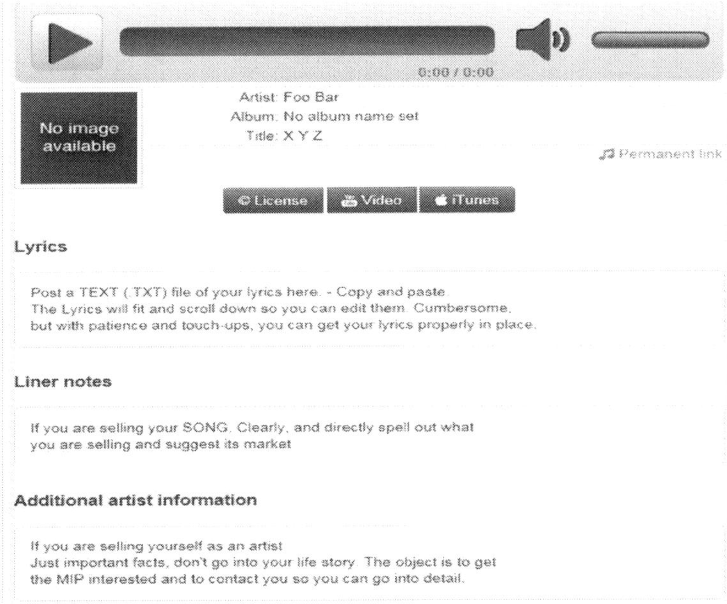

Now to proofread, proof-listen, and touch-up anything that needs it.

16. An Image would help your sales pitch, Let's add one.

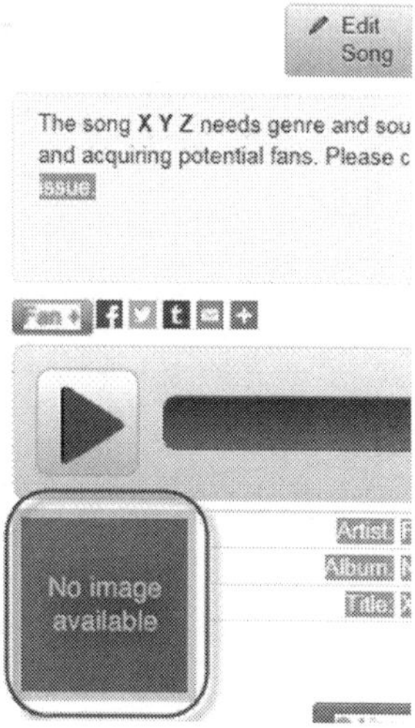

17. Select an Image from your files.

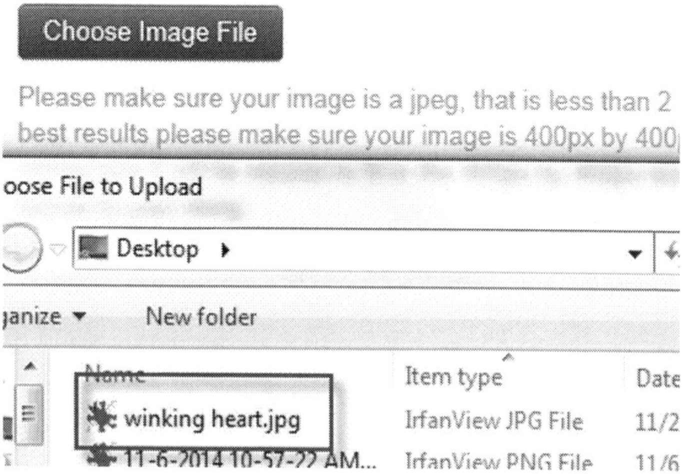

18. You will see "loading" for a minute or two as the image uploads.

19. Here's how it looks after the image upload.

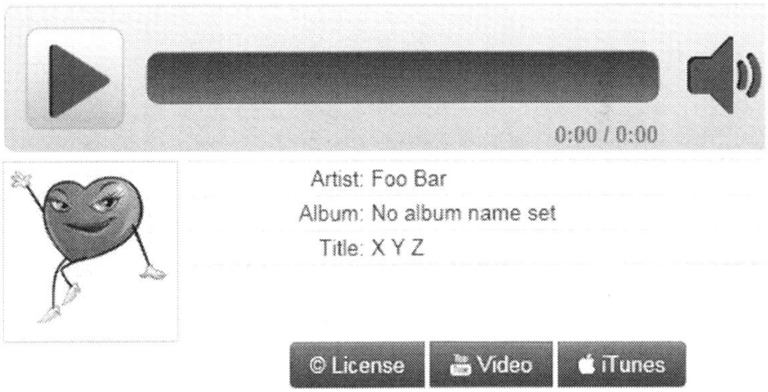

20. If you don't want to show an album name, replace the "No album name set" default with 3 blank spaces.

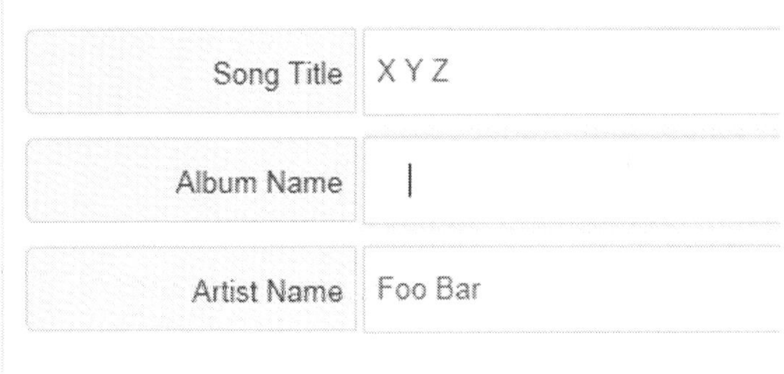

21. ... Now this is blank.

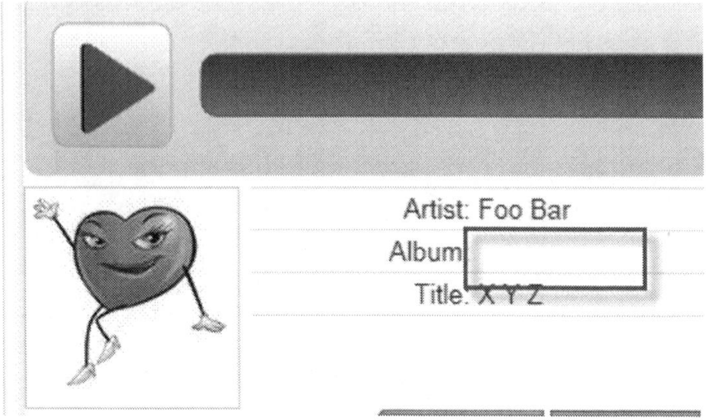

22. GET THE PERMANENT LINK to see the results.

23. This permanent link is a URL which is unique to your package. You can embed, email or whatever. This gives you a way to send <u>anybody</u> a SLICK LOOKING PACKAGE of Song, Lyrics and Pitch. All in one click. This is a valuable "hidden feature" you can put to use - even outside of MXR!

Your link will look something like this:

https://www.musicxray.com/xrays/7654321

24. And this is the finished look - as a MIP will see it.

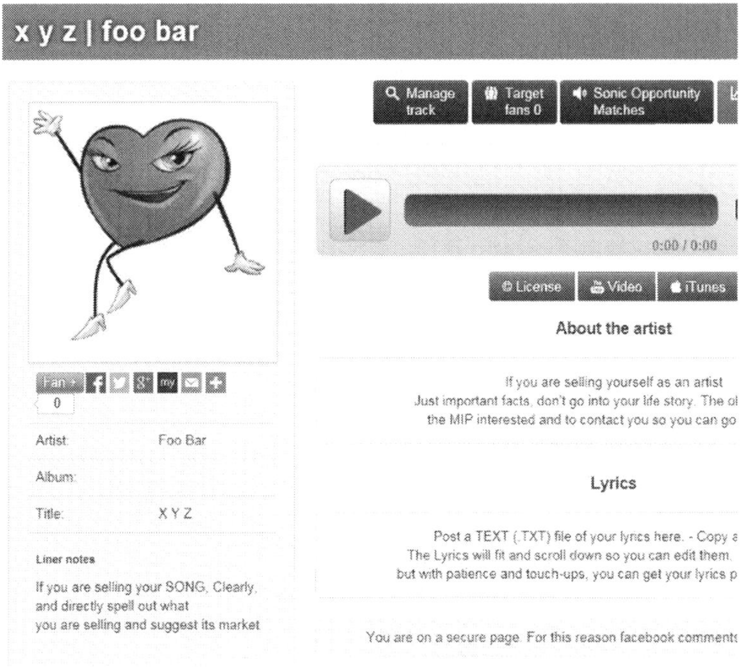

25. At this point – since you haven't purchased Diagnostics. If you wanted to, you could bail out and start over, at no cost.

26. BUT if all looks well (... perfect!) Click: "Get Music Xray Diagnostics".

And kick back and wait a few days till the critiques flow in.

Now that you have bought the Diagnostics, What do they mean?

XII. THE DIAGNOSTICS.

A lot happens on the Diagnostics page.

The most important is the matrix of evaluations by MIPs who have heard your song.

1. The "Ratings Received" scoreboard is the most valuable part of the process. Here is the picture writ large.

FRANKLY the gross truth seems to be.... If you can't show 18 stars, your song will have a rough time of it. If it shows 22 or more stars, you should easily find a buyer.

I've always thought these categories could stand a little improvement, because they don't tell the writer much that he can use to improve his product.

MXR is working on that but in the meantime, this may help you understand the objectives on which this process is balanced.

MXR offers you two kinds of "MIP": The Buyers and the Coaches. (See Below, the Coaches are 'boxed'.)

Labels / Record Deals	Collaborations
Top Industry Professionals	Compilations
TV and Movies	Contests
Artist Development	Distribution Deals
Artist Management	Exposure Opportunity
Artist to Artist Critiques	Featured Opportunity
Career Coaching	Festivals and Gigs
Celebrity Artists	Magazine/Print Reviews
Management Deals	Professional Song Critique
Marketing	Publishing Deal
Misc. Music Opportunities	Radio Playlisting
Music Blogs	Song placements
No Submission Fee	Songwriter Organizations
Podcast Inclusion	Sync licensing/Advertising
Production Deals	Sync licensing/General

MXR has located and persuaded the Buyers, the true "Ears" in the industry, to actually:

- Post Genuine Wants
- Honestly listen to submissions to determine if they fill the posted need, Yes or No. The Buyers aren't in the *How-do-I-help-this-writer-improve-his-song* business, that's a job for a Coach.

- The Buyer will give his opinion of the song by rating the factors that contributed to his decision. On a MIP-by-MIP basis, these ratings are highly subjective. That's why their overall average is more important.

You can learn a lot from the ratings, e.g., If a composition is rated low, while the production is 5 stars, you may be spending too much money demo'ing when you should be focused on re-writing.

Generally, MIPs who like a song, will give it a bunch of stars across the board, and vice versa.

The Coaches are a different matter. How they rate the song initially is not as important. You are paying them to tell you what the song needs, and how far it is from clearing the bar.

MXR does not want to burden a Buyer with the Coach's job. MXR must serve the Buyer as a conduit to the material that's "most likely to succeed"; otherwise the Buyers will seek a more fruitful, filtered source.

So MXR runs a reasonable compromise: the Buyer gets a more or less effortless way to listen to new material, and the Seller gets a true shot at ears he'd have a hard time getting access to. The 'shot' is the important thing, the MIPs' resulting Diagnostic ratings are a bounty to the writer

2. The Needle.

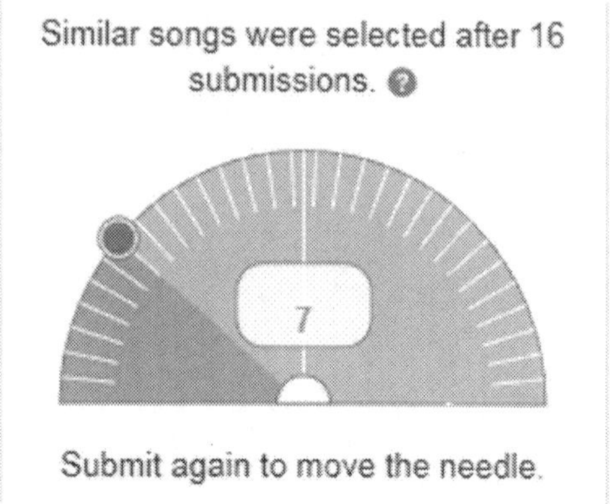

This is one of my few disagreements with the way MXR works. I think the "Needle" may be unintentionally misleading.

We see in the example a song which has been rejected 7 times, a forecast that: "Similar songs were selected after 16 submissions."

The forecast, based on a statistical pool, may be valid for the pool, but the writer can't infer, "WOW all I gotta do is keep hammering away at it 9 more times and it'll sell."

Before you take 9 more shots at a song, think about the Demo, the structure, and the target market - and maybe aim elsewhere.

(Seems to me, early on, I made about 30 submissions over about 9 songs and placed 4 of them. So in a sense 1 out of 8 was about right - overall. But it does not accurately tell the whole story, 4 songs got picked, 5 did not.)

All that said. I'd tend to discount the "Needle".

3. Fans of your song.

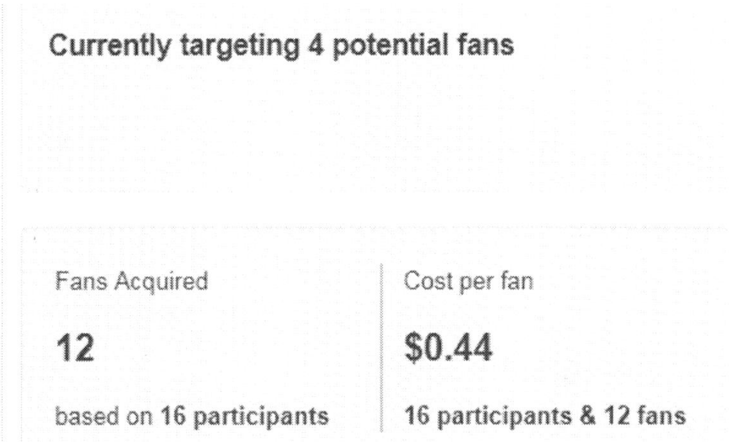

MXR Fans like to preview new material. In the Diagnostics, MXR sends a link to your song to 20 people in their database who are fans of the 3 "Similar To" artists you selected earlier.

Sometimes this process takes several days as the Fans get to their email inboxes. MXR will send your song to as many fans as necessary to get 20 like/dislike responses.

Here, 16 people heard it, 12 liked it and 4 did not. The "Cost Per Fan" indicator is, to me, as a writer who's not an artist, a bit meaningless. To my mind, the $10.00 Diagnostics' fee is buying the MIP's opinions. The Fan opinions are nice, but secondary to the Diagnostics process.

Interestingly, if the Fan response is LOW overall, and the MIP response is also LOW, I'd rethink the song, and maybe scrap it.

If the Fan response is HIGH even though the MIP ratings are low, I'd take a few more shots.

4. Fan Email Addresses.

One nice thing, MXR sends you the email addresses of the people who said they liked your song. They could be worldwide. As an artist, you are free to promote your performances, web site or products to them.

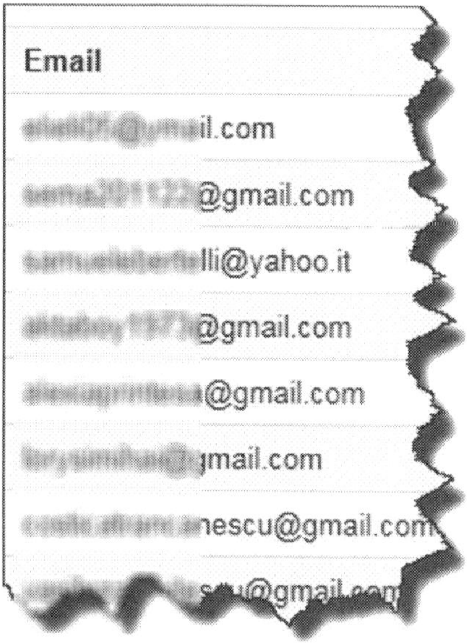

As a writer, sometimes an email interchange with an interested, objective listener, will tell you things about your work that all the coaching in the world might not uncover

Be sure to **download** and **save** this list of Fans.

5. The "Time Elapsed" meter.

This is basically just a feel-good pulse-beat of the system, to let everybody know the system is working and producing results.

(BTW, this does not count "Coaches", who are being paid specifically to comment. This only counts instances where the song is selected for use. These selections are across the board, from broadcasting on an internet special interest channel, to a release on a major label.)

6. The Song Activity Chart: A time line of your submissions and their outcomes.

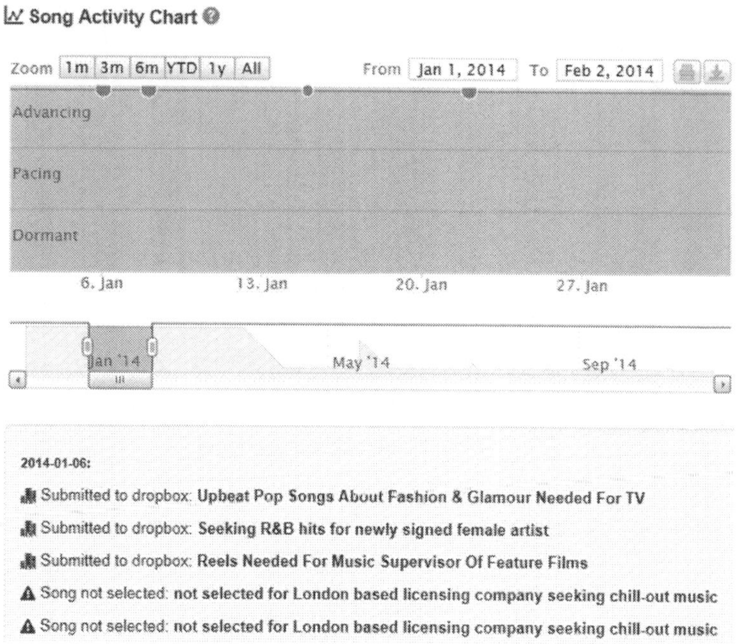

Here you can scan back over the history of your submissions and the industry's responses thereto. Each blue dot represents an event. Clicking on a dot will show you all the activity on that day - placement, acceptance or rejection. The time window is zoom-able, and the report may be emailed or printed out.

7. The List of Submissions and Results:

Here, in one place, you can see everything you tried and the results you got. Clicking on the listing will pop up full details of the dropbox to which you submitted.

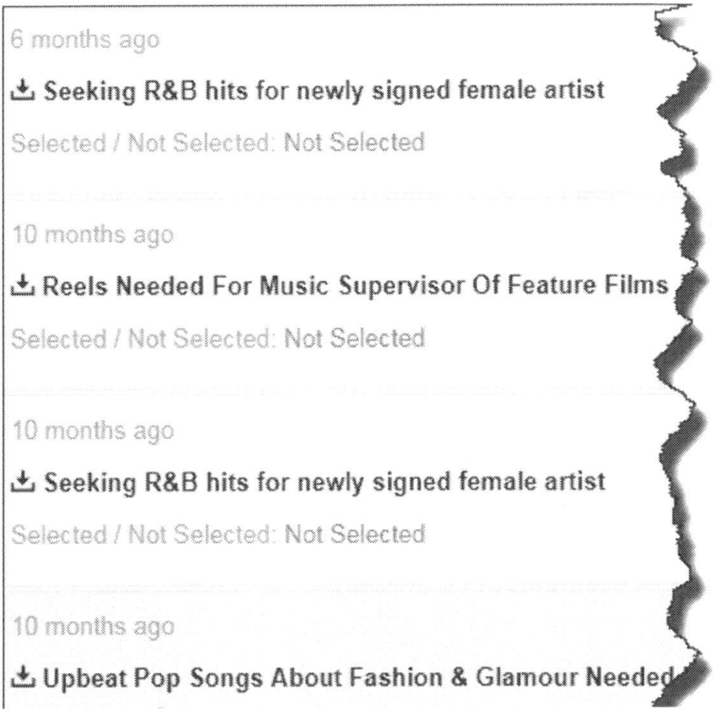

REMEMBER: You are only billed ONCE for the Diagnostics. Either voluntarily BEFORE you make your first submission, (I recommend this strategy,) or you are billed for the Diagnostics on the very first submission you make. After that you are only billed for the submission fees.

NOTE: The Diagnostics are not the "last word". But they do forecast the future more often than not. If your song returns very strong Diagnostics, you will most likely place it. If the report is weak, you may face a struggle. In all reality, rejections teach. Some people get "lucky", but true experience only comes from overcoming the weakness in the songs you get rejected.

Most songs which are rejected have some strong components. Strip mine the rejects for the good stuff and re-use it elsewhere.

And again. The true Outlier, The *Sine Qua Non*, the *Sui Generis* - The song you must pull over to the side of the road to hear because it is so good you can't even THINK...

...If you know in your heart you've written this, take your shot - regardless of what the Diagnostics might return.

Somewhere out there is a pair of ears listening for your heartbeat.

That's done.
NOW:
Where do I submit my song?

XIII. THE MIPs - THE BUYERS

MXR offers a lot of dropboxes, in a lot of categories. Many MIPs offer more than one box, each for a different need.

A dropbox can appear in more than one category, but you only need to submit your song once to a given MIP. Here's the list of MXR categories and some thoughts about them:

On MXR's site they are listed alphabetically, I've grouped them by general TYPE.

Labels/Record Deals - Song placements - Production Deals - Distribution Deals: These are the real target. Song in, Money out. Save your best shots for these

Sync licensing/Advertising - Sync licensing/General - TV and Movies: Probably the most fertile soil these days. Video and film needs a lot of music, if your song fits the producer's needs.

Publishing Deal: Ideally to hook up with a guy who'll get your song to one of the above guys.

Career Coaching - Artist Development - Top Industry Professionals - Artist to Artist Critiques - Professional Song Critique: These coaches will evaluate your song and give feedback. This is like psychotherapy, where the fit between the patient and the therapist must be right for maximum benefit to take place. The counselors are experienced and genuine. It may take you a couple of tries to find the one who really "speaks" to you and your writing.

Collaborations: This is generally not a specific writer looking for a collaborator. In many cases this is an offering by a publisher or producer for writers to work on staff or contract as part of a team of writer/producers.

(NOTE: Speaking of collaborations, the writer who is seeking a good new collaborator to work with via the Internet, can profit from becoming a "Fan" and listening to new material from new writers as it comes down the line. If you hear something appealing, contact the writer, start a dialog - who knows? You may find the perfect collaborator.)

Podcast Inclusion - Radio Playlisting - Exposure Opportunity - Compilations: If your music fits the theme of the show, you could get a wide preselected audience. Generally no payout, but exposure, and again... *Hey, you never know.*

Magazine/Print Reviews - Music Blogs - Marketing: Here, if selected, you and/or your music would be written up and featured in a publication or blog.

Contests: I'm always a bit wary of contests, because - particularly in the book business, the contest is sometimes nothing but a business operating on the spread between the total of the entry fees and the cost of the prize awarded. The "Merit" of victory can be questionable. That said, MXR does occasionally allow a MIP to post a contest. MXR researches the bona-fides of the MIP to be sure what is on offer is accurately described.

No Submission Fee: From time to time, often for charitable causes, a MIP will want music with no payout except exposure. You still pay MXR's $5.00 to submit, but no dropbox fee.

Featured Opportunity: This is simply a rotating, usually brand new dropbox which MXR is drawing to your attention. Often one with a short time window.

And all the OTHERS: Artist Management - Celebrity Artists - Festivals and Gigs - Management Deals - Misc. Music Opportunities - Songwriter Organizations: Generally postings in these categories will be duplicates of opportunities posted elsewhere.

Remember, MIPs are NOT allowed to use MXR to solicit business that requires additional payment or fees. If something appears unusual or improper to you, notify MXR immediately and they will either explain or remedy the situation.

XIV. YOUR SONG - AS THE MIP SEES IT

This is the Holy Grail. Now that you've come this far, here's the OZ-view behind the Emerald Curtain. This instructional video is what the MIPs are given to instruct *them* in how to USE Music Xray. It shows them how to stay on top of the flow of incoming songs.

The process is transparent, AND you can see directly how it rewards the active user with a "first look" at new, potentially hit, material.

The buyers want to buy somebody's music as actively as you want them to buy yours.

This is a MIP-view background video. It will give you a closed-loop understanding of how the process is cleverly balanced to cover every-one's self interest: **Yours, The MIPs, & Music Xray's.**

Viewing this is time well spent:

http://www.musicxray.com/How-Needlestack-Works

XV. SUBMITTING A SONG

This is far and away the easiest part of the whole deal. As you browse a category and see an opportunity which looks like your song might fit, click: "Submit to this Opportunity."

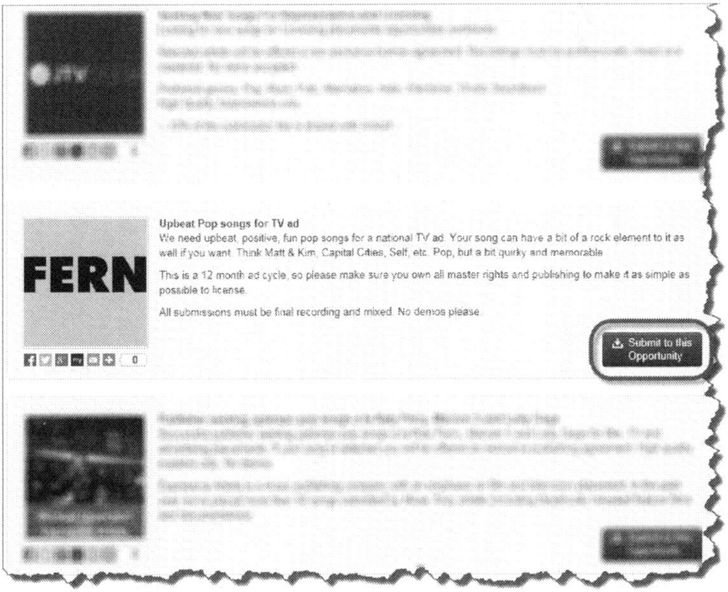

This will take you to a detailed presentation of the opportunity, and a profile of the MIP who is seeking the music....

... The Drop Box detail page.

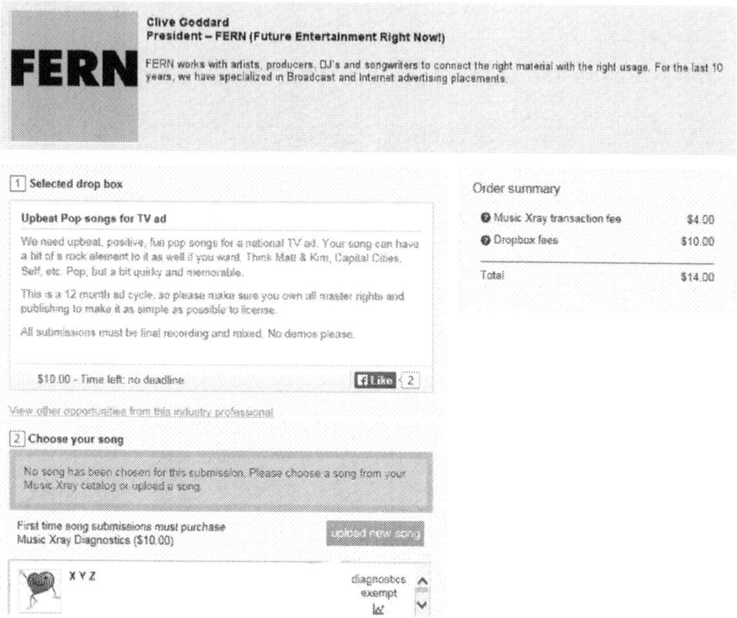

After you choose your song from your catalog you will see:

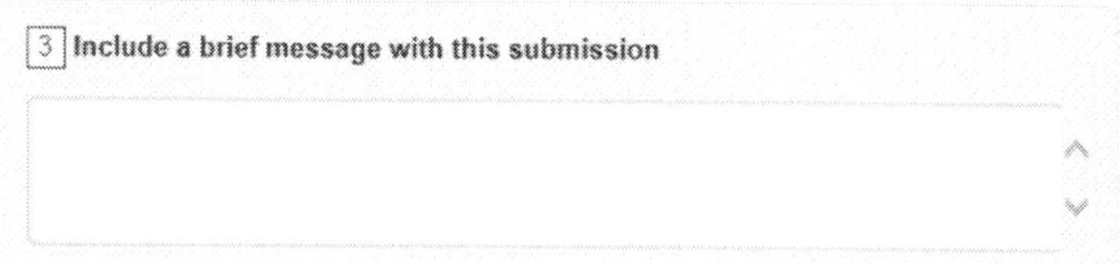

And I think "Brief" is the key word here. But BE SURE YOU'RE RIGHT - because once you hit "buy it" your package and message are off and running. May be a good idea to compose your message in NotePad, proofread it, and then copy it into place

Next you will see...The checkout button

You will have a chance to confirm the transaction before you are actually billed.

With this click, your song is in flight....
Hopefully to Ears that will get it cut, video'd, exploited, streamed and Grammy'd.

May we all be so rewarded!

XVI. PARTING THOUGHTS

A final "plug" here. Everybody who writes, or uses music, should be familiar with the "SGA Guild Contract"

> http://www.songwritersguild.com/sandboxs-ga2010/contract_primer_new.html

Originally created in the era of the "song shark". The scammer would post ads preying on little old ladies: "Your poem set to music". "Bing Crosby could sing your song." Then the up-sell, for demo money, promotion money, legal fees, etc.

The Guild, SGA (Songwriters Guild of America), has been populated by such heavyweights as Irving Berlin, Cole Porter, Rogers & Hammerstein, and Bob Dylan. It was founded to protect writers against sharks, low-lives and thieves.

Whether or not you use, (or get the publisher to use) the Guild Contract, you should read, learn and understand its terms. It's the Gold Standard contract for the writer. To me, it deprives the publisher of nothing, only requires him to truly perform as a publisher in order to own half of your song.

The most important language is the "Recapture Provision": The writers get their song back after a certain period of time if the publisher fails to get a recorded and released cut or meet some other contractual criterion.

Good Luck in your efforts with Music Xray. Stick with it. You'll learn which of your songs are great, because somebody will buy them … and you will learn which of your songs…. Well, you'll know…. *And let me know what I left out of this book. I'll add it to the next edition.*

All best,

Norman

Norman Dolph
Norman@GoodReadBooks.com

P.S. In case you're curious, I pay the same submission fees to MXR and the MIPS that you do.

APPENDIX: MUSIC XRAY - LINKS

Video Tutorial from MXR — The Big Picture:
https://www.youtube.com/watch?v=8bDsXcrpF7I

How Music Xray works for Musicians & Songwriters:
http://blog.musicxray.com/music-xray-works-musicians-songwriters-bands/

What is the background of the company?
http://www.musicxray.com/about-the-company

Success Stories:
http://www.musicxray.com/success-stories

FAQs:
http://www.musicxray.com/faqs

The Diagnostics:
https://www.youtube.com/watch?v=Rb_ykHqkvoo

The Stance Of The Company
http://blog.musicxray.com/credibility-matters-music-xray-good-true/

40419428R00060

Made in the USA
Lexington, KY
05 April 2015